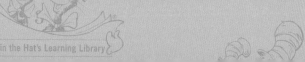

The editors would like to thank
BARBARA KIEFER, Ph.D.,
Charlotte S. Huck Professor of Children's Literature,
The Ohio State University, and
CHRISTINA COLÓN, Ph.D.,
Curator of Curriculum Development and Evaluation,
The New York Botanical Garden,
for their assistance in the preparation of this book.

Visit us on the Web!
Seussville.com
randomhousekids.com

Educators and librarians, for a variety of teaching tools, visit us at
RHTeachersLibrarians.com

Library of Congress Cataloging-in-Publication Data
Worth, Bonnie.
I can name 50 trees today! : all about trees / by Bonnie Worth ;
illustrated by Aristides Ruiz and Joe Mathieu.
    p. cm. — (The Cat in the Hat's learning library)
Includes index.
ISBN 978-0-375-82277-3 (trade) — ISBN 978-0-375-92277-0 (lib. bdg.)
1. Trees—Juvenile literature. I. Title: I can name fifty trees today!.
II. Ruiz, Aristides, ill. III. Mathieu, Joseph, ill. IV. Title. V. Series.
QK475.8.W67 2006 582.16—dc22 2004028626

Printed in China
40 39 38 37 36 35 34 33 32 31 30 29 28 27 26 25

I Can Name 50 Trees Today!

by Bonnie Worth

illustrated by Aristides Ruiz and Joe Mathieu

The Cat in the Hat's Learning Library®

Random House 🏠 New York

I'm the Cat in the Hat
and I want you to please
take a few moments
to look at the trees!

If you pay close attention,
you might get to exclaim,

"There are 50 trees
I bet I can name!"

7

A tree is a plant
with a stem made of wood.
Do you know what a stem is?
A trunk! Very good.
Some trees grow to 10
or to 20 feet high.
Some grow till their tops
scrape the clouds in the sky.

98 FT.

PECAN

DEVIL'S WALKING STICK

30 FT.

10 FT.

FLOWERING DOGWOOD

A cypress in Mexico
that we have found
has a trunk more than
117 feet round!

BALD CYPRESS

A tree in Australia,
the land that's down under,
stands 492 feet tall—
oh my, what a wonder!

EUCALYPTUS

The branches grow upward.
The roots they grow down.
The branches and leaves
are what we call the crown.

Some crowns are like cones
(like this cute little fella).

Some crowns match the shape
of my nifty umbrella.

AMERICAN HOLLY

SUGAR MAPLE

AMERICAN ELM

WEEPING WILLOW

Some, like this willow,
droop down to the ground.

Some, like this apple tree,
are nearly round.

APPLE

WHITE OAK

I'd say this white oak is
as wide as it's tall,
while this pine doesn't have
low branches at all.

RED PINE

11

JAPANESE MAPLE

Let's look at the roots.
We will speak of them first.
They hold the tree up and
they help quench its thirst.

They draw water up
and, science has found,
they even draw minerals
out of the ground.

SHOOTS

BRANCHES

LEAVES

The trunk and the branches,
the leaves and the shoots,
bring water and minerals
up from the roots.
The leaves then pull off
one tree-mendous feat.
They whip up the food
that the tree needs to eat.

SIBERIAN ELM

They mix water up
with rays from the sun,
add carbon dioxide and
when the leaf's done . . .
it gives off the oxygen
we need to survive.
(It's a gift from the trees
that keeps us alive.)

Here's a fast grower
(this will surely amaze ya).
Over one inch each day
this tree grows in Malaysia!

While way up in Canada
a four-inch slowpoke
is 155—
I tell you no joke!

ALBIZIA
FALCATA

ATLANTIC
WHITE CEDAR

THING
1

Some leaves are so simple—
one leaf to each stem.
While others have
leaflets growing on them.

PRICKLY ASH

"LEAFLETS"

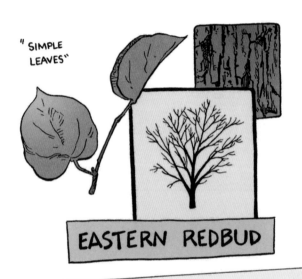

" SIMPLE
LEAVES"

EASTERN REDBUD

Some leaves grow on stems
in these neat little pairs.

SILVER MAPLE

"PAIRED LEAVES"

"LEAFLETS"

HORSE CHESTNUT

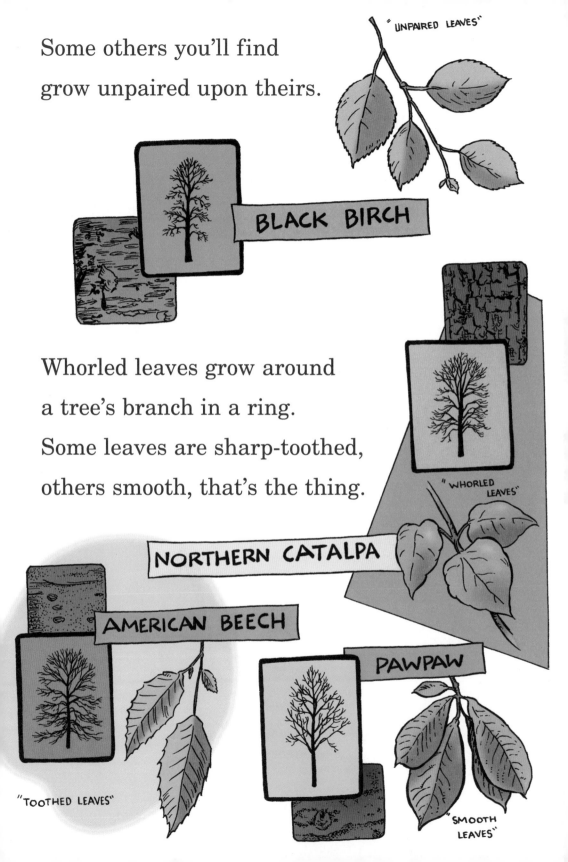

Some others you'll find
grow unpaired upon theirs.

"UNPAIRED LEAVES"

BLACK BIRCH

Whorled leaves grow around
a tree's branch in a ring.
Some leaves are sharp-toothed,
others smooth, that's the thing.

"WHORLED LEAVES"

NORTHERN CATALPA

AMERICAN BEECH

PAWPAW

"TOOTHED LEAVES"

"SMOOTH LEAVES"

Like your ears, some have lobes,
which means that they are
shaped a lot like your hand,
or a mitten, or star.

SWEET GUM

SASSAFRAS

FIELD MAPLE

19

Bark does for a tree
what your skin does for you:
stops the weather, the bugs,
and the germs getting through.

REDWOOD

The bark of the redwood,
you have to admire,
is two whole feet thick
and protects it from fire.

The bark of this tree
is what has made it famous.
Shagbark hickory is what
this shaggy tree's name is.

SHAGBARK HICKORY

A neat trick a friend of mine
just showed to me
is to find out the age
of a once-living tree.

A new ring is added
with each living year.
Let's count up the rings
in this stump over here.

A year that has rain
leaves a ring that is thick.
This thin ring means drought
(or our poor tree was sick).

We've counted and we'll
share our answer with you.
It's 67—
did you find this was true?

23

SAPWOOD

HEARTWOOD

BARK

OLDEST-KNOWN
LIVING TREE

24

The oldest tree ever
(and this one is fine)
might be 4,700 years old—
a bristlecone pine.

BRISTLECONE PINE

CAVE THING 2

There are all types of trees.
But of course you knew that.
One has needle-shaped leaves
or scales that are flat.
Its seeds come in pinecones,
so let's be exact
and say it's a conifer—
yes, that's a fact.

NEEDLE-
LEAFED
TREES

LARCH

WHITE PINE

SPRUCE

HEMLOCK

EASTERN RED CEDAR

JUNIPER

SARGENT CYPRESS

ARBORVITAE

SCALE-LEAFED
TREES

27

Another type, broadleaf,
you've probably seen
in the fall turning colors
and losing its green.
The seeds from these trees
come in nuts that are hard
or in soft or dry fruits like
in Sally's backyard.

BLACK WALNUT

PAPER BIRCH

SWEET CHERRY

RED MAPLE

"MAPLE FRUIT"

And then there are palms.
They grow where it's warm,
with leaves like a feather
or fan-like in form.

COCO-DE-MER

The world's largest seed,
from the coco-de-mer,
weighs 50 whole pounds.
Things, you'd better beware!

ROYAL PALM

Forget not the lily trees,
lovely to see.
Like this king of the desert,
the Joshua tree.

JOSHUA TREE

If you ever get burned,
then you had better go
get the leaf of the yucca
that we call aloe.

YUCCA

The tree fern is oldest
and, what is more,
it doesn't have seeds.
Instead, it has spores.

The tree fern fares better
in much warmer weather.
This tree's rather short
with a leaf like a feather.

TREE
FERN

SPORES

The cycad is old
and, for what it is worth,
there were cycads when
dinosaurs once roamed the earth.
 It looks like a palm,
 but a palm it is not.
 How long is its cone?
 Three feet long! That's a lot!

SOUTH
AFRICAN
CYCAD

CONE

33

The tree called the ginkgo,
we've saved for the last.
The first one grew 250
million years in the past!

GINKGO

One thing that I think
you should know about ginkgo—
its fruit doesn't smell good.
In fact, it smells stinko!

Get yourself a blank book
to press leaves that you find.
Glue them onto the pages.
Your mother won't mind!

Note the tree's bark
and the shape of the crown.
Note the shape of the leaves
and then write it all down.

Take a look at this book
or get a tree guide.
Match up your leaves
to the pictures inside.

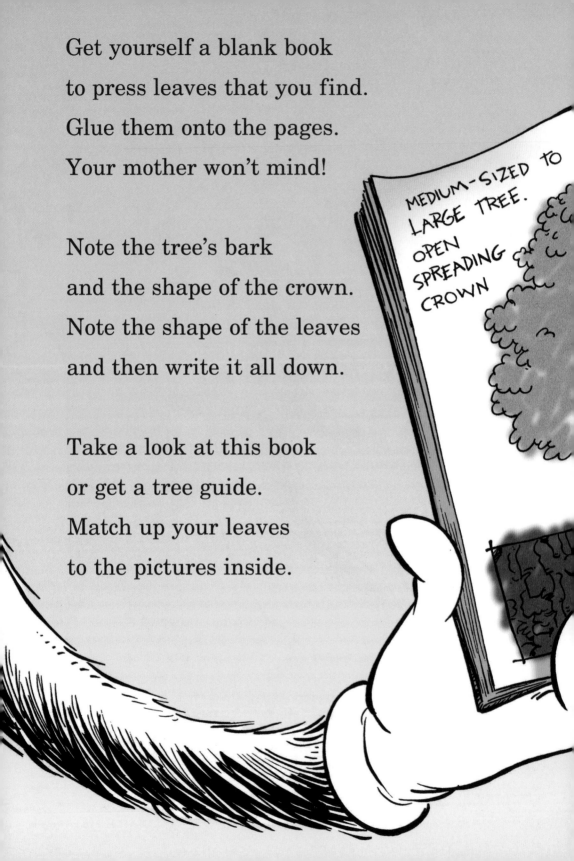

MEDIUM-SIZED to
LARGE TREE.
OPEN
SPREADING
CROWN

Write down the tree names
and learn them by heart.
This book contains 50
and that's a great start.

Knowing trees' names,
my dear miss and dear mister,
is like knowing the name of
your brother or sister.

We can't have enough of these
wonderful trees.

So when you see bare spots . . .

... go plant a tree, please!

GLOSSARY

Drought: A time during which no rain falls, which is difficult for plants and animals.

Germs: Tiny living things, too small to see with the naked eye, that can cause sickness or disease.

Heartwood: The innermost part of the trunk of a tree, which no longer carries sap.

Lobes: Curved edges (such as on leaves) that stick out.

Minerals: Natural substances found in the ground that plants absorb to help them grow strong and big.

Quench: To bring to an end—as in to quench a thirst by taking a drink.

Sapwood: The soft, living part of the trunk of a tree, which lies between the inner bark and the heartwood.

Spores: Tiny grains given off by some plants or trees that make new plants.

Whorled: Spiraling out from a central point.

FOR FURTHER READING

Be a Friend to Trees by Patricia Lauber, illustrated by Holly Keller (HarperCollins, *Let's-Read-and-Find-Out Science*®, Stage 2). Learn all about the amazing ways trees provide food, shelter, and other necessities. For kindergarten and up.

The Lorax by Dr. Seuss (Random House). The classic rhyming tale with a powerful environmental message. For kindergarten and up.

Tell Me, Tree: All About Trees for Kids by Gail Gibbons (Little, Brown Books for Young Readers). All about the life cycle and parts of a tree. For kindergarten and up.

Tree by David Burnie (DK, *Eyewitness Books*). Amazing photographs show the life of a tree. For grades 4 and up.

A Tree Is Nice by Janice May Udry, illustrated by Marc Simont (HarperCollins). Discover all the fascinating things trees can do! For preschool and up.

INDEX

Albizia falcata, 15
aloe, 31
American beech, 17
American elm, 10
American holly, 10
apple, 11
arborvitae, 27
Atlantic white cedar, 15

bald cypress, 8
bark, 20–21, 24, 36
black birch, 17
black oak, 37
black walnut, 28
branches, 10, 11, 14, 17
bristlecone pine, 25
broadleaf trees, 28

carbon dioxide, 15
coco-de-mer, 30
cones, 26, 33
conifers, 26
crown, 10–11, 36
cycads, 33

devil's walking stick, 8

eastern red cedar, 27
eastern redbud, 16
eucalyptus, 9

field maple, 19
flowering dogwood, 8

ginkgo, 34

heartwood, 24
hemlock, 26
horse chestnut, 16

Japanese maple, 12
Joshua tree, 31
juniper, 27

larch, 26
leaves, 10, 14, 15, 16–18,
    26, 30, 32, 36

minerals, 12, 14

northern catalpa, 17

oxygen, 15

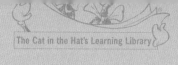